Alice Appleby
And
The Kirkham Bum Blasters

By N. B. Fletcher

Copyright © 2023 N. B. Fletcher
All rights reserved.
ISBN: 978-1-3999-7367-0

For Alice, The Kirkhams, and the infamous
Bum Blasters

CONTENTS

1	Stargazing	Pg 1
2	Breakfast Seed	Pg 5
3	The Kirkham Bum Blaster	Pg 9
4	Lady Melantha Blagden	Pg 13
5	Cooking Up A Storm	Pg 18
6	Christmas Day	Pg 28
7	Test Blasts	Pg 33
8	Travelling Bums	Pg 37
9	Farting All The Way	Pg 42
10	Wonderland Paris	Pg 47
11	The Short Fart Home	Pg 50
12	Missing Formula No.3	Pg 54
13	Moonlings	Pg 60

1. STARGAZING

The stars twinkled and winkled against the fabric of night. With not a cloud in the sky, the moon shone clear and bright. A Hunters moon, according to Alice's Dad. It was the kind of night Lucky the Cat stayed out until dawn.

Grandad looked up at the moon. "Can you see it?" He asked. "The craters and how wonderful and detailed everything looks? It's like you could reach out and touch it."

Alice peered through the telescope's eyepiece. "It's moving quite fast. I can only see an edge. It's out of focus."

"So it is," said Grandad, taking control of the telescope and adjusting it for Alice. After a short while, he handed it back. "The moon has to be fast; it's chasing the sun."

"Wow, I can see it now!" said Alice excitedly. "It's so clear I can see every crater, but there's almost no colour at all."

"That's right. It's just light and darkness. Each crater is where an asteroid has collided," said Grandad.

"Wow," said Alice, looking in wonder at the moon. "And it's all made of cheese?"

"Every bit of it," chuckled Grandad. "You know Alice, there's a man that lives on the moon. It's his job to make sure mice don't eat it."

"Wow! Doesn't he get lonely, up there by himself?" asked Alice.

Alice Appleby And The Kirkham Bum Blasters

"I suppose he must." Replied Grandad, looking up at the moon wistfully.

To Alice, it looked like a fine place for an adventure. Who wouldn't want to go somewhere with as much cheese as anyone could wish to eat? I wonder if they have a chocolate moon too, thought Alice.

Shortly after, the cold became too much for the two stargazers to bear. They retreated inside to warm themselves with mugs of hot chocolate by the fire. Then, to their beds they went, tucking themselves into their thick duvets and the safety of their dreams.

* * *

At the break of dawn, before anyone else was awake, Alice heard scratching from downstairs. She ventured down to the kitchen and opened the door, letting in Lucky the Cat. A heavy dew hung from the plants and cobwebs. To Alice's surprise, the telescope was still outside.

They must have forgotten to take it in with them the night before, thought Alice. Why don't I bring it in now? Slipping on her sparkling, pink wellies, she stepped out into the garden. She trod cautiously over the wet grass before reaching the old, wooden bench where the telescope had fallen on its side.

Without thinking, she put her eye to the eyepiece of the telescope and peered in. At first, everything was blurry and out of focus. Feeling around and finding the adjustment wheels, she began twisting them until the telescope's view came into focus. Instead of the starry sky like the night before, the telescope focused on a little house on a hill. To Alice's surprise, she saw another telescope and a person peering straight back at her.

She was not prepared for this so early in the morning. Pulling back from the eyepiece, she felt a tingle of fright prickle all over her body. She looked at the house in the distance, then peered back into the telescope. The person in the house on the hill was gone.

"Alice! You'll catch your death of cold!" came the telling voice of Mum. "Get back inside this instant!"

"But Mum, I just wanted to get the telescope," said Alice, doing her best to explain why she was out in the garden so early.

"Alice, leave it where it is and get inside. Grandad will get it later."

Alice did as her mum asked, hopping carefully back over the wet grass to the safety and warmth of the house. The telescope rescue would have to wait for Grandad.

2. BREAKFAST SEED

It wasn't long before the Appleby household had woken up. Breakfast was in full swing with toast, scrambled eggs, and cereal being handed about.

Grandad and Dad both loved scrambled eggs on toast. Dad liked his covered in lashings of ketchup, whereas Grandad covered his in brown sauce. Once a month, Grandad would have a terribly smelly, smoked kipper, and Alice would have to hold her nose to keep the stench out. Grandma liked cereal with lashings of milk on her wheat biscuits, rice snaps, or cornflakes, and Mum liked toast with jam.

Alice liked to mix it up. Sometimes, she'd have egg, but other times it might be one of the cereals, or maybe toast and jam. However, she would never have a kipper! Pongy! This morning was toast with lashings of butter and strawberry jam.

As Grandad finished his scrambled eggs, Alice decided now would be a good time to tell him about his telescope.

"Grandad, I went out to get your telescope from the garden this morning, and when I looked through it, I saw a person looking back at me from the house on the hill."

"The house on the hill?" asked Mum.

Then, Grandma spoke. "Oh, that house. That belongs to Lady Blagden. She's a terrible woman! Only after money and power. She thinks everyone else is beneath her. She even thinks she should be Queen! Her family used to own all the land around here, but they have long since sold it. For years, Lady Blagden has been trying to get everyone to pay her money for living here. She's bad news. Just make sure you

Alice Appleby And The Kirkham Bum Blasters

stay away from her Alice."

Grandad piped up. "Well, thank you for trying to rescue my telescope, Alice. I'll have to fetch it in after breakfast."

Everyone sat quietly for a moment, eating breakfast. Dad had already finished his and began to sort through the morning mail.

"Alice, it looks like you have a package!" said Dad, handing it to her across the breakfast table.

A package? Who could that be from? thought Alice.

"It looks like your Auntie Kimberley's handwriting," said Mum.

They all watched with interest as Alice gently tore the top of the package. In it was a little notebook and a card. As Alice opened the card, a little folded paper packet slid out onto the table. On it was written, *Kirkhams Bum Blaster Super Seed*.

Alice began to read the handwritten card from Auntie Kimberley.

Dear Alice,

I'm sorry I've not been able to visit. I'm writing to you from the deepest depths of the Peruvian Jungle. I'm on an expedition to find rare and exotic plants. We've come across a new type of chili plant with extraordinary powers. Local, tribal elders swear by them as a method of supreme transport.

The Kirkhams chili seeds are incredibly rare, but they have special qualities that make them super. I can't go into too much detail now, but I've sent you a single Super Seed to grow. Please keep a note of how the Chili grows in the enclosed notebook.

Look out for a letter from me near Christmas. There will be further instructions on what to do with the Chili's. Hopefully, I will see you soon.

Love and Hugs,
Auntie Kimberley xxx

Alice held up the paper packet, and through the morning sunlight, she could see the faint outline of a single, tiny seed.

Mum took the card and read it to herself. "A Super Seed? We can find a pot and plant it together later."

Alice nodded in agreement, crunching on the last of her toast and jam.

After breakfast had been cleared away, Alice put on her sparkling pink wellies and went into the garden to pick out a little clay pot from a pile of unused pots behind the shed. Mum carried in half a bag of compost and laid it on the kitchen table. Together, they planted the single, Kirkhams Bum Blaster Super Seed.

Mum suggested putting it by the kitchen window so it would keep warm and get enough light to grow, so that's where the pot sat.

3. THE KIRKHAM BUM BLASTER

Alice visited the little clay pot every morning before breakfast to give it a little water, hoping to see the seed begin to grow, but for weeks, nothing happened.

"Oh, come on plant. Please grow!" implored Alice.

Another week passed and still no sign of a plant.

"I don't think it's germinated. The seed might have rotted," said Mum, looking at the empty pot. "If it doesn't grow soon, we might just have to throw it away."

"Oh, please don't throw it away! I'm sure it's not rotten. I'm sure it will grow," begged Alice. She desperately wanted the little plant to appear, because she knew Mum wouldn't let her keep an empty pot on the side for too much longer.

That night before bed, she visited the little pot on the kitchen window. "Oh, little Super Seed. I do wish you would grow! I know you can grow up to be a Super Plant!"

The very next morning, Alice came down to check on the little clay pot and give it a drink of water. To her surprise, instead of an empty pot, a tender, green shoot had appeared in the middle of the dark compost.

"Mum, Dad, Grandad, Grandma. Look! It's started to grow!"

The Applebys gathered around the little clay pot to marvel at the green shoot that had appeared.

"You'll have to give him a name," said Grandad.

"I'll call him Alfred," said Alice. And so, the little chili plant was named Alfred. Alice noted down the name in the little notebook.

Alice Appleby And The Kirkham Bum Blasters

As the weeks passed, Alfred the chili plant grew and grew. Leaves soon appeared, and Alfred occupied almost the whole of the kitchen window.

One morning, Alice came to give Alfred his daily water, when to her surprise, she noticed little red and purple flowers had appeared.

Aren't they wonderful?" said Alice. "Look, there are eight in total."

"They're fantastic!" said Mum. "And what a lovely smell! Why anyone would ever call them Bum Blasters, I don't know."

Another couple of weeks passed, and the petals from the eight flowers curled up. In their place, little green chilis had started to grow.

"Mum, Dad! Look! It's growing chilis!"

"Oh, how wonderful!" said Mum.

"Do you think the chilies will be ready soon?"

"Auntie Kimberley said they would be ready just before Christmas," said Mum.

All but one of the eight green chilis grew a little bit bigger each day. Alice knew because she had started to measure them with Dad's tape measure and note the exact measurements in the little notebook. The one chili that didn't grow much, if at all, sat at the very top of Alfred. It had begun to shrivel in on itself. "That one must be a little bit poorly," said Alice to Mum.

"Well, you have seven other fine chilies growing, and look at that one at the bottom! It's going to be huge!" said Mum.

"That's the Super Chili! I think it's extra special," said Alice with a smile.

"Is it really? I don't know what we're going to do with them when they're fully grown. I suppose we could cook them up for dinner one night. I know a great recipe for chili con carne," said Mum.

"No, Mum! They're special! We've got to wait for Auntie Kimberley! She said she'd send me a letter with instructions nearer Christmas," said Alice.

"Well, let's hope Auntie Kimberley doesn't get lost in the jungle!" said Mum with a laugh.

Alice knew Auntie Kimberley wouldn't get lost in the Jungle. She just had to keep a close eye on Alfred and make sure the chilies kept growing.

* * *

Later that day, Grandad was sitting in the living room watching TV, when an advert popped up that caught his attention.

"Look Alice, come quick!" he cried pointing excitedly at the TV. Alice ran as fast as she could into the Living room, but she was just too late. The advert had ended.

"Too late, you missed it." Said Grandad.

"What did I miss?" asked Alice.

"It was an advert for a new Amusement Park."

"What's an Amusement park?" asked Alice.

"It's a place that has lots of fun things to do! There are rollercoasters, and rides of all sorts! And in the very middle, there's a big Castle!" said Grandad.

"That sounds fun! I've always wanted to see a Castle!" said Alice.

"Well, this Amusement Park is called Wonderland Paris. If you're lucky, your Mum and Dad might take you!" said Grandad.

"I do hope I'm lucky," said Alice.

"You'll have to wait and see," said Dad, popping his head around the Living room door. "Paris is quite a long way away, but if you're a good girl, then maybe your Mum and I will take you!"

"Well, I am good, and I'd love to go!" said Alice with a big grin. She knew Dad was more than likely already planning to take her there!

Alice thought Wonderland sounded great! Who wouldn't want to go on an adventure to Paris, riding on rollercoasters and seeing a Castle? She decided to note down Wonderland in her little notebook, as a place she'd like to visit one day.

Alice Appleby And The Kirkham Bum Blasters

4. LADY MELANTHA BLAGDEN

It was the end of summer, and Alice had long forgotten about the incident with the telescope when she had seen a person looking at her from the Blagden's house on the hill. And why would she remember that on a beautiful, sunny day like today? She was much more interested in playing with Lucky the Cat and some string in the back garden.

But Lucky had other ideas. With a flick of his tail, he hopped up onto the fence and over to the little country road that ran alongside the Applebys house.

"Oh, Lucky!" said Alice. She knew she wasn't allowed out of the garden by herself, but if she was with Lucky, she would be fine, wouldn't she?

So long as I don't go too far, I won't get in trouble, Alice thought to herself.

Alice pushed open the little white picket gate and ventured out. Lucky had been drawn to the butterflies flitting and fluttering among the flowers that grew along the hedgerows on the opposite side of the road. Where Lucky went, Alice soon followed.

The butterflies danced and swung little cartwheels in the breeze mesmerising Alice. So much so, that she nearly didn't notice a fast-approaching car until it was almost upon her!

The car whizzed past, missing Alice by inches, and the screeching sound from the brakes made her jump for her life! Luckily, her fall was cushioned by the hedgerow, and she was fine apart from a bit of dirt and a few twigs tangled in her hair.

Alice had never seen a car like this one before. It was very large and grand, and it was sparkling white as if it were made from one million tiny diamonds all squashed together. In the front, it had a large, shiny, metal grill with a little metal angel. And the roof, well it didn't have a roof at all. That's when Alice noticed the occupants.

In the driver's seat sat a little man in a green uniform and a matching cap, and in the back, a beautiful woman with jet-black hair. The woman's lips curled up slightly as if she were about to give a command.

Without saying a word, the little uniformed man got out of the driver's door and unfolded a little step. Opening the passenger door, he said, "We have arrived m'Lady."

"Thank you, Gawk," said the beautiful lady, curling her lips again. Gawk held her hand as she used the step to exit the car. She wore a long maroon dress and had a matching handbag.

Alice picked herself up from the hedgerow and began to dust herself off. She barely had a chance to untangle the twigs from her hair before she noticed the Lady and Gawk staring at her.

"Look m'Lady, a horrid child! It has twigs in its hair and dirt on its face!" exclaimed Gawk.

"Oh, how awful! It looks bedraggled!" laughed the Lady.

Gawk joined in on the laughter.

"I'm not a horrid child! And anyway, it's your fault I look like this. You almost ran me over!" cried Alice in the most unimpressed voice she could muster.

"Serves you right you filthy, little brat! Perhaps your parents hate you, and that's why they let you play on the road!" sneered Gawk.

"I'm not a brat! And my parents love me! They tell me I'm wonderful!" screamed Alice.

"Get it away from the car, Gawk. Before it leaves a mark," commanded the Lady with a backward waft of her hand.

"Get away vile, little rodent," snarled Gawk as he moved towards Alice with his hands reaching out to grab her.

Alice Appleby And The Kirkham Bum Blasters

"I beg your pardon!" Came Mum's voice from across the road. Her voice was enough to stop Gawk in his tracks. Alice's Mum stood at the white picket gate outside the Appleby house.

"Who gave you permission to talk to my daughter like that?" continued Mum.

Gawk steadied himself. Standing upright to face Mum, he composed himself and put on the fakest of smiles. "This is Lady Melantha Blagden of the Blagden Estate," he said, gesturing to Lady Blagden. "And I am Gawk, her manservant."

"Well, I'm Mrs. Appleby, and you've no right to talk to my Alice like that! Come on, Alice," said Mum.

Alice ran across the road and to Mum's side.

"Oh, so she's your daughter? How delightful to make your acquaintance Mrs. Appleby. Although, I hear a rotten apple doesn't fall far from the tree," said Lady Melantha Blagden, stalking her way across the road.

"She is my daughter, and the only thing that's rotten around here is you," said Mum defiantly.

Lady Melantha's lip upturned in a horrible sneer. "Enough talk. Deliver the letter, Gawk," commanded the Lady.

Gawk hopped across the road and slid the letter over to Mum.

"The Blagden Estate owns part of the land your house is built on. As such, there's an estate fee of one thousand pounds you must pay every year. As the fee hasn't been paid for many years, the amount you owe the Blagden Estate is now over ten thousand pounds, plus interest. Payment is due the day after Christmas."

"But we can't possibly afford that! And at Christmas? Who collects money at Christmas?" asked Mum, opening the letter and reading it.

"It's all explained in the letter. We'll come to collect on Boxing Day. Find a way to pay! And if you can't pay, we'll take something away!" smiled Gawk with a horrible smile.

Mum just stood there in silence reading the letter.

"Gawk, enough. Onwards to town. Leave the simpletons to earn their keep," said Lady Blagden, getting back into the rear of the car.

Gawk jumped in the driver's seat and the sleek, white car zoomed off into the distance.

Alice and her Mum went back inside the house and hugged. A little tear rolled down Mums cheek.

"Promise me you'll stay away from that Lady Blagden and her horrible manservant," said Mum.

"I promise," said Alice.

So, Lady Melantha was the person I saw through the telescope, thought Alice to herself. What nasty people.

Later that evening, just before bed, Alice overhead her Mum telling Dad what had happened.

"We can't possibly pay! And we won't! It's illegal! There's absolutely no truth in the letter – they don't own the land our house is built on! And they have no right to exploit us for living here!" said Dad angrily.

"I do hope you're right, dear," sobbed Mum. "In any case, it's probably best we save our money. We'll have to cancel our holiday to Wonderland and cut back on Christmas presents this year."

"You're right dear. I just hope Alice understands."

Alice made her way upstairs. She didn't mind if they didn't have any presents at Christmas, or if they never went to Wonderland, so long as Mum, Dad, Grandma, and Grandad were happy. That's what mattered most.

At least I have Auntie Kimberly's letter to look forward to. I do hope it turns up soon! Thought Alice to herself.

5. COOKING UP A STORM

Autumn came, bringing with it Halloween Pumpkin carving, then fireworks night with big bangs and colourful displays. Then, after no time at all, the nights drew in, and it became very cold outside.

Dad and Grandad put up the Christmas tree. Lucky then pulled down the tree, and it had to be put up again and redecorated. The Applebys only set of lights was carefully wrapped around the tree, and all different types of ornaments, old and new, hung on the tips of its branches.

Alfred the chili plant had lost all but three of his leaves, and the chilies had started to turn purple with yellow stripes.

It was precisely one week before Christmas. It was the exact time Alice expected a letter to arrive from Auntie Kimberley, but at breakfast, there were no letters for Alice, just one letter addressed to her parents. She was beginning to think it would be best if Mum just chopped the chilies up for dinner. After all, if Auntie Kimberley wasn't going to tell her what to do with them, why let them go to waste?

Alice stirred her spoon around the bowl of cereal. Her eyes came to rest on the letter addressed to her parents. She recognised the posh swirly handwriting on the front. The letter was from the Blagdens! She watched as her Dad opened the letter and began to read. Mum looked over his shoulder intently, trying to see what the letter contained. Dads cheeks grew a little red, and his eyebrows became taught with anger.

"Alice, please can you go to the living room. Your Mum and I need to talk."

Alice knew this was serious, but she wanted to know what her parents were going to say. So without a word, she got up and left the kitchen, closing the door behind her. Then, she turned and pressed up her ear to the door to listen in on her parents conversation.

"The Blagdens can't still be trying to charge us for living here!" said Dad putting the letter down on the table with a bang.

"What'll we do? It says they'll come to collect on Boxing day." said Mum

"I don't know how we could possibly afford to pay them."

"We've got our savings. We could always pay them from there. And we won't be going to Wonderland, so that will save us money."

"We'll have to cancel Christmas!" said Dad.

"Oh, don't say that, dearest husband! How about we don't invite Auntie Lori and Uncle Paul to Christmas dinner, that's two less people we have to feed. And we're off to the market this afternoon. If we're frugal, we can buy just enough food to have a Christmas dinner and afford to pay the Blagdens a little."

"And what about presents?" asked Dad

"We'll just have to skip presents this year. After all, they're not that important. So long as we have each other."

"I guess you're right," said Dad.

Alice quickly ran to the living room and no sooner as she sat on the sofa, Dad opened the door to the kitchen.

Alice turned her thoughts back to the letter from Auntie Kimberly. It was only after breakfast that a knock on the door came. A delivery driver delivered a rectangular parcel packaged in brown paper and string. Mum brought it in and put it on the table in the kitchen. The Applebys gathered around. They hadn't had a parcel delivered in months. Since the letter from Lady Blagden, they hadn't been able to afford hardly anything and had been saving their pennies.

"It's addressed to you, Alice," said Grandma.

Alice felt everyone's eyes turn to her. "Whatever could it

be?" asked Alice.

"Best open it and find out," said Grandad.

Alice came over to the table and carefully undid the white string, then started to peel at the corners of the parcel.

"I'll get some scissors. It'll be quicker," said Mum. She was right. In no time at all, the brown paper came away to reveal a wooden box. The lid of the box lifted up to reveal three different-sized, glass flasks, a set of glass vials, and a set of eye droppers. The contents were held in place by a protective foam casing.

How strange, thought Alice to herself.

"Look, Alice! It's a letter!" said Dad.

"It's from Auntie Kimberley," said Mum, holding the letter up. "You can tell by the writing!"

Alice opened it carefully. This time it was a Christmas card with a picture of a chili plant covered in Christmas lights, but there were no little folded paper packets of seeds. Instead, there were three pieces of lined paper, each with a list of instructions.

Alice began by reading the card:

Dear Alice,

Sorry for being unable to visit you. I am still deep in the Peruvian Jungle! I have spent time with the local Medicine Man, learning to unlock the powers of the chili plant and its secrets of transportation. I'm pleased to say we've had an amazing breakthrough! We now know the secrets of the Kirkham Bum Blasters!

Hopefully, you have been able to grow a Kirkham Bum Blaster chili plant from the seed I sent you in my last letter. If you were successful, you will be able to follow the enclosed formulas to make your own Bum Blaster! I have also sent you an early Christmas present. It's a set of the finest flasks and vials to help you store the final formulas.

Remember, you must use the chilies before Christmas, otherwise, they may not work as intended. Also, for best results, you must leave the formulas to settle for precisely one week before using them.

The best of luck! Get cooking!

Auntie Kimberley

P.S. Look out for the Christmas presents from me! They should be arriving soon!

Alice took out the three pieces of paper containing the formulas. "Mum, Auntie Kimberley gave me formulas for super chilies! Can you help me cook them?"

"Alice, I've been thinking about the chilies. Maybe it's not a good idea to cook them. They don't sound very safe."

"But they're from Auntie Kimberley, and I'm sure she wouldn't send me anything dangerous."

"I know, but maybe it's best we wait for Auntie Kimberly to come here in the summer. Then you can make the formulas together. Besides, we're about to go to the market to see if we can find something to eat for Christmas dinner. So we won't have time to make them now anyway."

"But Mum! Auntie Kimberley said we *have* to make them now!" cried Alice.

"Well, I've decided it will have to wait until Auntie Kimberly gets here."

Alice crossed her arms and marched into the living room, where Grandad had already begun to fall asleep in front of the TV. She didn't want to go out in the cold to the silly market. She decided that if she was going to make formulas, she would have to do it herself.

Alice waited patiently for Mum, Dad, and Grandma to leave the house. Immediately she gathered Auntie Kimberley's formulas and the wooden box containing the flasks and vials and took them into the kitchen. Then, she found three different-sized pans and a large wooden cooking spoon. After moving one of the kitchen chairs over to the cooker, she stood on it and lined up the pans by size.

"Let's start with Formula Number One!" Alice said to herself, looking at the ingredients.

> **Formula No. 1 Mild Bum Blaster - Super Taste**
>
> **Ingredients:**
> - Three cans of fizzy pop
> - One bowl of Rice Snaps
> - Five assorted chocolates
> - Vanilla essence
> - One tube of glitter
> - One large chili - biggest available
>
> **Instructions:**
> Start with three cans of fizzy pop on medium heat. Stir in the Rice Snaps and chocolate, then add a splash of vanilla essence for flavour. Chop the chili up finely, then add to a pan. Continue to simmer for fifteen minutes or until the colours stop pulsing.

Taking the scissors, Alice carefully cut free the largest Chili, the Super Chili, away from Alfred the plant. Then, she found a can of fizzy, orange pop and some Rice Snaps. These were the easiest ingredients to get. Now, on to the tough ones. She took the remaining chocolate from her advent calendar and poured it into the first pan, then she turned on the heat. But she didn't have any vanilla essence. "I'll just have to use brown sauce!" she said. So, she took the brown sauce Grandad liked and squirted that in.

The mixture fizzed and bubbled away, and Alice stirred it until a wonderful yellow and purple colour pulsed throughout the mixture!

"This is brilliant! On to the next formula! Formula Number Two," said Alice to herself.

Formula No. 2 Bum Blaster

Ingredients:
- Two cans of fizzy pop
- Five pickled onions
- Ten brussels sprouts
- Two whole eggs
- A sliver of cheese
- A pack of bubble gum
- One large smelly sock - used
- Six chilies (except the smallest, most shrivelled chili)

Instructions:
Start with the fizzy pop on medium heat. Pop in the onions, sprouts, eggs, and cheese. Packet and all. Add bubble gum for consistency, then drop in the chilies whole and stir counter-clockwise for one minute. Continue to cook for one hour or until the formula turns blue.

That's easy, thought Alice to herself.

She carefully pulled a sock from Grandad's foot as he snored. The six chilies were easy to snip off, and the other ingredients were easy enough to get, although she had to search her Dad's spare coat pockets to find some chewing gum, which was the nearest thing to bubble gum Alice could find.

Before using the chilies, she scraped a couple of the Kirkham Bum Blaster seeds into a piece of paper and folded them up, just like how Auntie Kimberley had sent her the original Super Seed.

"I'll be able to grow more Kirkham Bum Blasters next year!" thought Alice to herself.

The mixture fizzed and bubbled away, and Alice stirred it for one minute, but which way was counter-clockwise?

I'm sure it doesn't matter that much, thought Alice to herself. On to Formula Number Three.

Formula No. 3 Bum Blaster Rocket Fuel - Do Not Use!

Ingredients:
- The smallest, most-shrivelled chili - chop finely
- Half a bottle of ketchup
- Cornflakes
- A smelly fish
- One large smelly sock - used

Instructions:
Throw everything into a pan and leave to simmer down for one hour or until the formula turns completely black. This formula belongs to NASA, the National Aeronautics and Space Administration. Do not ever use this formula. It is advanced and potentially dangerous! Keep it in a safe place, and I will collect it and take it to NASA when I come to visit in the summer.

This is the easiest of the lot! thought Alice. She carefully pulled the other sock from Grandad's foot as he slept and took a smoked kipper from the fridge. She then tossed them in with the cornflakes, half a bottle of ketchup, and the last remaining shriveled-up chili from Alfred. She monitored the formulas to ensure they were all behaving themselves.

Formula No. 1, the Mild Bum Blaster, was ready first. The colours had stopped pulsing yellow and purple. Alice set it aside to cool. Next, was Formula No. 2, the Bum Blaster,

Alice Appleby And The Kirkham Bum Blasters

which turned blue. Then, Formula No. 3, the Bum Blaster Rocket Fuel, which turned completely jet black.

After leaving the formulas to cool, Alice poured each one carefully into the glass flasks, and then sealed them with cork stoppers. She washed up the pans and wooden spoons, and she cleaned down the sides of the sink so it would look as if nothing had happened.

Then, she took the glass flasks upstairs, along with the wooden box containing the other equipment, and put them under her bed for safekeeping.

Alice sat back down in the living room next to Grandad, who was still fast asleep. A minute later, Mum, Dad, and Grandma arrived home.

"Hi, Alice. You didn't miss much, but we did get our food for Christmas dinner!" said Mum.

"You're back quick!" said Grandad with a yawn.

"We were gone ages. What have you done with your socks?" asked Grandma.

"Oh, must have forgotten to put them on," said Grandad, a little confused.

Alice smiled. She had gotten away with making the formulas on her own. Now, all she had to do was wait one week, and then she could use them!

6. CHRISTMAS DAY

It was Christmas morning on the twenty-fifth of December! Alice rushed downstairs, and to her surprise, under the tree were loads of presents! But they seemed to be bigger this year than last year! This year, there were seven large presents.

"Wow! I didn't think we were getting presents this year!" said Alice excitedly. She tried her best to read the labels on the nearest present, but before she got the chance, Mum interrupted.

"Now Alice, you remember the Appleby present rule. No presents until after Christmas dinner!"

Alice nodded and sat down to watch the TV.

This year, Mum and Dad were making Christmas dinner. There was a small turkey with as many trimmings as they could afford, stuffing balls, pigs-in-blankets, roasted potatoes, carrots, brussels sprouts (yuck), and parsnips.

It was also precisely one week from when Alice had cooked the formulas. As Auntie Kimberley had said, it was now safe to use them. But how could she do it?

A little thought began to worm its way inside her head. Maybe I could put some of the formula in the Christmas dinner! Only a little! Then, I could observe what happens.

So that's exactly what Alice decided to do. She ran upstairs and took out the glass flask from under her bed: Formula No. 1, Mild Bum Blaster!

Mild Bum Blaster can't be too bad, can it? If anything, it must surely be a good thing! thought Alice. She took the cork out and filled up one of the little glass vials with the formula.

She slipped it into her pocket, pushed the wooden box back under her bed, and went back downstairs to where Mum and Dad were making Christmas dinner.

"Mum, Dad, Can I help with dinner?" Alice asked.

"Oh, I don't know. We've got everything in hand," said Dad.

"Alice, you can take out the gravy to the dining table," said Mum, pointing to the gravy boat that sat on the kitchen table. "Then, after dinner, you can tell me all about what happened to the Alfred the Chili plant." She said looking at Alice knowingly.

Mum must know I've made the Bum Blaster Formulas! If so, she might stop me before I get a chance to use them. It's best I take my chance and use one of them now! Thought Alice to herself.

She smiled at Mum, then took the gravy boat and carried it carefully through to the dining room. Making sure nobody was looking, she reached into her pocket and retrieved the glass vial containing Formula No. 1. She carefully poured it into the gravy and swirled it around with her finger. Then she put the gravy boat in the middle of the table, where everyone could reach it.

It wasn't long before the rest of Christmas dinner was ready. The Applebys each filled their plates in the kitchen and took them to the dining room.

Alice watched as the gravy boat was passed around and poured onto each of the dinner plates. She pulled out her little notebook to take notes. The same notebook she had used to note the growth of the chilies and the formulas from Auntie Kimberley.

"Mmm, isn't it lovely? It tastes like honey and nectar. Not at all like a Christmas dinner, but it is wonderful!" said Grandma, eating the food covered in Gravy.

"Honey and nectar," said Alice, noting down the reaction.

"It's amazing! The most delicious food I've ever tasted!" said Grandad. *Amazing*, wrote Alice.

Oh, it is wonderful!" said Mum. Alice added another note

in her notebook. *Wonderful.*

What a success! She thought to herself. If only she had a way for someone to try out Formula No. 2! But as luck would have it, she didn't have to wait very long. Dad hadn't had any of the gravy yet.

Alice watched him from across the table. His eyes were searching for something.

"Where's the horseradish sauce?" asked Dad.

"It must be in the fridge," said Mum.

This was Alice's second chance of the day. "I'll get it for you Dad!" said Alice.

She dashed from the table, up the stairs, and pulled out the wooden box from under her bed. Uncorking the flask of Formula No. 2, she took an eye dropper and carefully drew up the smallest of blue droplets. Then, she put the box back and took the eye dropper with Formula No. 2 downstairs to the fridge. Taking the lid from the horseradish sauce, she pressed the eye dropper, making the little, blue droplets trickle onto the sauce. Then, she mixed it all together using a teaspoon and carried the sauce to the dinner table.

"Here you are, Dad," said Alice with a smile, and she sat down at her place with her notebook at the ready.

"Thank you, Alice!" said Dad, taking the lid off the horseradish sauce.

Alice watched as Dad retrieved a large dollop of sauce using the teaspoon and smeared it all over his roasted potatoes. She wondered if it might have a bad taste. After all, it did contain pickled onions, brussels sprouts, and one of Grandad's used socks! But adults like that kind of food, and in any case, she didn't have to wait long to find out. Dad took his first bite of a roast potato smothered in horseradish sauce.

"Scrumptious!" he said, taking another bite, then another in quick succession. *Scrumptious,* noted Alice.

"This is delicious!" he said through another mouthful. "What did you add to this?" he asked.

"Oh, just Formula No. 2, Bum Blaster," said Alice quietly, while jotting down another note.

"You didn't," said Mum glaring at Alice.

"I did," said Alice with a smile.

Both Mum and Alice turned to look at Dad. He was gulping down his dinner so fast, it was as if he had never eaten before, and as he got to the end, he licked the plate clean.

"My goodness! That was the best Christmas dinner I've ever eaten!" he said.

"You shouldn't have put that in," said Mum to Alice.

Everyone at the dinner table had stopped eating and was listening intently to the conversation.

"Nonsense!" said Dad. "Is there any more?"

"Well, Bum Blaster Formula No. 2 is actually in the horseradish sauce," said Alice.

"Is it really?" said Dad, picking up the jar and putting his finger in to fish some out.

"What's that funny ticking noise, my dearest?" said Mum.

Everyone looked at Dad. A tick, tick, tick could be heard from his belly. His face began to turn purple, and his eyes began to swell like they were going to pop. The ticking got louder and louder, and then he began to vibrate and ting. He was like a human alarm clock going off.

POP WHHOOOSHHHH!!!

A gigantic fart blasted, with a bright, red flash from Dads bottom, sending him flying up into the air, up to the ceiling. He looked like a Firework that had been lit!

"HEEELLLLLPPPP!" he screamed. But there was nothing that could be done. For a moment, he was out of control, whizzing around the room like a balloon that had been let go! Then after what seemed like a minute, the firework noise stopped, and he fell back down to Earth.

Mum rushed over to Dad's side and, thankfully, he was okay. The Applebys sat in silence for a couple of minutes.

It was Bum Blaster Formula No. 2. They all knew it.

Alice Appleby And The Kirkham Bum Blasters

7. TEST BLASTS

Dad had locked himself in the toilet and refused to let anyone in. Mum leant up against the door trying to coax him out. Alice jotted down in her notebook that it was a little after 3 pm. It was important to capture all the data she could about such a marvelous event.

"I can't believe you would pull such an awful trick on your poor Dad. It's wicked!" said Mum to Alice.

"It wasn't a trick. I didn't mean any harm! It was just an experiment," said Alice innocently.

"It's Auntie Kimberley's fault. She's to blame with her Kirkham Bum Blasters!" said Grandma.

Mum whispered through to the toilet door. "Are you all right, darling? "

A flushing sound could be heard, and a moment later, Dad appeared.

"Of course! I'm fine! Never better!" said Dad with a smile that beamed from ear to ear.

"We thought you might be in shock," said Grandma, looking at him suspiciously. After all, he'd been flying around the Christmas dinner table!

"Shock? No! I thought it was amazing! The best fun I've had in years, and it felt fantastic! It's the first time a man has flown by his own wind! His own steam! Well, fart-steam! The only thing I have to ask is, have we got any more?" said Dad with a smile.

"Well, I do have some more as it happens," said Alice. But before she could explain further, Grandma interrupted.

"Oh no you don't! Dad, don't encourage her. It's

dangerous!" said Grandma.

"Besides, you can't fly now. It's time to open the Christmas presents," said Mum.

So, the Applebys gathered around the Christmas tree, and Alice started to read the labels on the presents.

"Looks like Father Christmas has been good to us this year!" said Grandma as Alice handed a present to each of the Applebys. These were the presents from Auntie Kimberley. There were also two similar-looking presents from Uncle Paul and Auntie Lorri, but because they were not here this Christmas, Alice put their presents to one side.

It wasn't long before the Applebys had started to tear off the wrapping paper. Alice unwrapped hers. At first, it looked like a large, pink backpack, but it didn't have any zips, just a cord that you pulled and some safety straps. The rest of the Applebys had the same type of backpack, although a little larger than Alice's.

"These are parachutes," said Grandad knowledgeably.

"Parachutes! Whatever are these for?" asked Grandma.

"Is there a card from Auntie Kimberley? That's sure to tell us what these are for!" said Mum.

But there wasn't a card. While the other Applebys were in deep discussion about the parachute presents, Dad and Alice slipped away. Alice retrieved a vial of the Bum Blaster No. 2 from her bedroom. She met Dad back in the kitchen, where he had begun to strap on the parachute.

"So, what we'll do is a test flight to see if it's safe!" said Dad.

"What does it feel like?" asked Alice.

"It feels amazing! Like you're flying! I can't wait to try it again," he said.

Grandad appeared at the kitchen door. "Can I help?" he asked.

"Of course," said Dad.

Grandad went over and adjusted the safety straps on Dads parachute, and then the three of them went outside and into the garden.

"I'll test it first to make sure it's safe, then we should all try a little trial flight," said Dad.

"You only need a little to set off," said Alice, using her eye dropper to put a couple of drops of Formula No. 2 on a sugar cube.

"Let's do it," said Dad, taking the sugar cube and putting it in his mouth.

The ticking noise came, and then, with a flash, he blasted up into the air.

"He's gone quite far," said Grandad, looking up.

"I think he's stopped," said Alice.

"Who's stopped?" asked Grandma. Alice turned and saw Grandma and Mum standing by the backdoor.

"Dad," said Alice, pointing upwards.

They all watched as the parachute opened, and Dad glided gracefully down to the end of the garden.

"It's fantastic!" yelled Dad. A few minutes later, the parachute had been packed away, and the Applebys were back inside the house, gathered around the kitchen table.

"We've got to go somewhere!" said Dad to the rest of the Applebys.

"What if the Blagden's come for their money, and we're not here to give it to them?" asked Mum.

"Forget about the Blagden's! They won't come to collect money at Christmas! Anyway, we could be in North Pole, or sunning ourselves in Spain for all they know!"

"He's right, you know. They won't come to collect at Christmas, so we might as well go somewhere. Maybe somewhere hot!" said Grandma hopefully.

"I think we should let Alice choose where we go. After all, it's her formula," said Grandad.

"Well, Alice, where would you like to go?" asked Mum.

Alice thought for a moment, and then an idea popped into her head.

"Wonderland Paris! We can go on all the rides, and see the castle, and it will be so much fun! Oh, please can we go?"

Alice Appleby And The Kirkham Bum Blasters

"Wonderland Paris? Well, it's a full day if we go there. We'd have to leave early in the morning," said Dad.

"We could leave tomorrow! First thing on Boxing Day!" said Grandma.

"Great, so we're all agreed. First thing tomorrow morning, we're off!" said Dad.

And so, the Applebys went to bed early that night.

Just like that, the destination was set. They were going to Wonderland Paris.

8. TRAVELLING BUMS

The next morning, Alice awoke early. A thin dusting of snow had fallen overnight, and the air had a freezing feeling to it.

After a very quick breakfast, the Applebys made their way out to the back garden, forming a queue next to the old wooden table where the gifts from Auntie Kimberley and ten vials of Kirkham's Bum Blaster No. 2 sat. Alice had used her eye dropper to make sure each vial had the same amount. She used every last drop of Bum Blaster No. 2, so their trip had better be worth it!

Dad and Grandad stood at the front doing final equipment checks. Every strap had to be checked and double-checked. There was little room for any mistakes.

It was freezing cold for Boxing Day, and everyone had on their gloves, coats, and scarves. Alice wore her pink and red scarf and sparking wellies. Grandad and Dad both had on their big winter coats, and as for Grandma, she had on three extra layers of jumpers!

Mum appeared wearing what looked like a hoodie, two coats, and three scarfs, with another in her hands.

"Alice, you're not wearing nearly enough warm clothes!" she said, proceeding to put one of the scarves over Alice's head.

"But Mum!" said Alice in protest.

"You can never be too warm on a winter's day like today," said her mum, ignoring Alice's protests.

"Right, I think we're ready!" said Dad excitedly, standing up on the table so everyone could see him.

"Now, everyone, I know this is the first time we've ever tried this as a group, but it's been so long since we went on holiday, and Auntie Kimberley seemed certain it would work, so I think we should all just give it a go! Before we proceed, does anyone have any questions?"

Grandma's hand shot up.

"Yes, Grandma," said Dad.

"How do we know where we're going?"

"Great question. Grandad has a map, so what we'll do is let him go first, then we'll all follow!"

All eyes turned to Grandad, who smiled and waved a map in his hand.

"But what if we get separated?" asked Mum.

"Another great question! To stop ourselves from getting separated, we'll tie ourselves together with a piece of rope. That way, we'll all stick together, and no one will get lost."

"But won't the rope get in the way when we need to land?" asked Grandma.

"When we fly over our destination, we'll simply let go of the rope, then we can set off our parachutes and land safely! Now, does everyone know how to set off their parachute?"

Alice's hand shot up. "Yes, Alice," said Dad. All eyes turned to Alice.

"You pull the special cord!" said Alice with a smile.

"That's right! Well done!" said Dad. "Now, does anyone else have any questions?"

Everyone looked at each other for a moment.

"Great! Let's prepare for take-off!" said Dad excitedly.

First, the parachutes went on, then Grandad did a safety check on everyone to ensure the parachutes were fastened correctly.

"Now remember, when we get up in the sky, I'll tie a special knot in this piece of rope that will tie us all together. When we're above our destination, pull this piece here and it will unravel and free you from the rope," said Dad to Alice.

After a few minutes, everyone had their equipment on and had been safety-checked by Grandad.

It was time to take Kirkham's Bum Blaster No. 2.

Grandma handed out the little vials. Two for each of them. One for the journey to Paris, and one for the return journey home. "Keep the second one safe, otherwise you'll be stuck in France!" said Grandma, handing two vials to Alice.

A cold gust of wind sent a shiver across the group. Standing in line, everyone took their first vial and removed the cork stopper. Alice could have sworn the mixture fizzed and changed colour a little when her cork was removed.

Dad turned to look at everyone. "We'll take it together on three. One ... two ... three!"

The liquid hit the back of Alice's throat, fizzing and whizzing its way down into her stomach. It felt like drinking pure excitement, and the taste was wonderful, like caramel and fresh lemon cheesecake, but with a zing! The excitement in Alice's stomach didn't stay there for long. It started a warm, rumbling feeling like one thousand wild horses wanting to escape. Her body began to move like it was doing a funny dance. For a moment, she wondered what she had just done, but it was too late. She couldn't undo it now.

Looking over at Grandma, Mum, Grandad, and Dad, she saw they were all doing a funny dance too. Grandma's face had turned bright red. Then the ticking sound started.

"Oh no," she said. A flame leapt from her bum and sent her up into the air.

Pop, pop wooooshhhh!

The smell was foul, like rotten, pickled eggs! "Phewww," said Alice, holding her nose. Grandad was next, with his red face and his bum firing. Then, in a flash, Mum's bottom exploded behind her, sending her flying into the sky.

Only Dad and Alice were left to go. Like twin rockets, they held hands, and farted in unison, soaring high, hot on the heels of the other Applebys.

Alice Appleby And The Kirkham Bum Blasters

9. FARTING ALL THE WAY

Up, up, and away flew Alice and her Dad through the thick, fluffy, grey snow clouds. Soon, they were so high there were no clouds left. Instead, they were surrounded by bright, blue sky and the cold glare of the winter sun. The other Applebys were circling above, waiting for them.

Alice thought farts blasting out of her bottom would be painful, but if anything, it felt absolutely delightful! Like her whole body was being propelled by thousands of invisible, little hands, pushing her along.

The farts were tremendously powerful, and they each left a white fart trail. Alice soon realised she didn't ever want to cross paths with the fart trails if she could help it. The smell was nothing short of atrocious!

"Erghhhh! It's like a cross between pickled herrings and rotten eggs!" she said to Dad as he blasted across her path.

"Sorry!" said Dad, looking back.

"More like a skunk who ate a rotten brussels sprout! Or sewers on a particularly hot day!" said Grandma, holding her nose.

"You know, I think it has a hint of fish and sweaty, smelly socks!" said Grandad.

"Definitely smelly socks!" laughed Alice.

"That one smelt like a dog fart!" Said Grandma, holding her nose.

"Right, everyone. Grab hold of the rope, that way we won't get lost," said Dad, passing the rope behind him.

Mum, Grandma, then Grandad grabbed hold of the rope.

"Come on, Alice! It's your turn to grab on!" said Dad.

Alice blasted a little faster to catch hold of the rope.

"It's a little bit chilly up here, and we can't even see where we are on the map," said Grandad.

"The clouds are in the way. Let's fly back down, beneath them, and then we can get our bearings. On three, everybody!" said Dad. "1 … 2 … 3!"

The Applebys began their descent through the clouds, being careful not to go too fast in case they accidentally hit the ground.

Grandad took the lead with his map in hand. "Okay, I can see where we are. If we follow this motorway, then we'll get to Dover, and then we should be able to find our way to the coast. We'll cross the English Channel, and with any luck, we'll be able to see all the way to France!" said Grandad.

So, they bum-blasted away, following the motorway so fast, that their cheeks began to wobble against the cold north wind.

This must be what a jet pilot feels like, thought Alice to herself.

"Does anyone know any good songs? asked Grandma. "I usually listen to the radio when I'm in the car, but we don't have a radio."

"I know one. It's called Jingle Smells, Sing along with me!" said Dad. Then he began to sing:

"Blasting through the snow,
on a wild and windy day,
Making bad smells as we go,
Farting all the way!
Farty, Fart, Fart!

Oh, jingle smells
Your family yells,
Phew, please go away!
Oh, what fun it is to fly
On a wild and windy day! Hey!

*Jingle smells,
Your family yells,
Phew, please go away!
Oh, what fun it is to fly
On a wild and windy day!"*

Mum, Dad, and Grandad were laughing, but Grandma didn't look very impressed. "You're all a bunch of children!" she said.

"I've got one," said Grandad with a giggle.

"Don't you dare sing it," said Grandma disapprovingly, but that didn't stop Grandad.

*"We wish you a smelly Christmas,
We wish you a smelly Christmas,
We wish you a smelly Christmas,
And a farty new year!"*

Alice couldn't help but laugh.

Grandma was about to say something when Mum shouted, "Look! It's the coast!"

Mum was flying slightly higher than the rest of the Applebys, so she had a slightly better view. She was right. A blue line, followed by a thin, yellow line, had appeared on the horizon. In almost no time at all, the thin line of sand grew bigger and bigger, and then they were flying over the sand. Looking down, they saw it wasn't only sand, but also giant, white cliffs.

"We'll be able to use them as a reference point on our way back!" said Dad to Alice.

They farted on across the blue sea of the English Channel. Below them passed all sorts of boats, from fishing boats, to oil tankers, to cruise ships, to great, big container ships.

Alice's favorite was a giant passenger ferry. She and the rest of the Applebys waved at the passengers as they flew by. People ran out on deck to take pictures and wave back.

Alice Appleby And The Kirkham Bum Blasters

"They can scarcely believe their eyes!" said Mum.

"Grandad, stop showing off," said Grandma. Grandad had let go of the rope and was circling above doing loop the loops!

"Just having a spot of fun!" cried Grandad.

"That looks like great fun!" said Alice, and she let go of the rope to do a giant loop the loop! Then, the rest of the Applebys joined in!

"Come on, we've got to get to Wonderland before our farts run out!" said Dad. "Follow me!"

They farted along the French coast and blasted their way up the River Seine. Soon, they were flying over the city of Paris.

"Turn right at the Eiffel Tower!" cried Grandad with the map in his hand. Despite it being Boxing Day, the Eiffel Tower was packed with visitors, and Alice did her best to wave at them as they blasted past.

"How much further do we have to go?" asked Mum.

"We're almost there. Look, there's the castle!" said Grandad.

"That's good. I think I'm about to run out of … oh," said Mum with a wobble.

Alice looked back at her. The bum blasts had started to run out! "Oh no! Come on, Mum. We're almost there!"

Grandad and Grandma came to the rescue, picking Mum up by her arms.

"We're here! Time to set off the parachutes!" yelled Dad. He was right. The Wonderland castle was right in front of them. Grandma and Grandad let go of Mum, and then all of the Applebys let go of the rope they had been holding on to.

Alice felt herself falling through the air.

"Remember to pull the cord, Alice!" yelled Dad as he fell.

Alice yanked on the cord to her parachute. She felt a light tug on her back, as the parachute canopy released, and then the falling feeling turned into more of a floating feeling.

Together, the Applebys floated to the ground, landing right outside the Wonderland castle.

10. WONDERLAND PARIS

Within ten minutes of landing, the Applebys had packed away their parachutes and dropped them off at the Wonderland Paris luggage storage.

"Right, what rides are we going on first?" asked Grandma.

"Pirates of Atlantis!" said Alice.

"Lead the way! I need some rum!" said Grandma excitedly.

So, the Applebys went on the Pirates of Atlantis ride. Not everything went as expected. Bum Blaster Formula No. 2 had some unexpected side effects: huge farts! But if there's one thing about the Applebys you should know, it's that they never admit to breaking wind.

The first unexpected side effect happened when one of the Pirates appeared. Grandma accidentally let one rip. The puff of wind from her bottom bowled over the Pirate!

"Oops, that wasn't me!" said Grandma.

"It was! I can't believe you'd lie about something like that!" laughed Alice, but Grandma just smiled and didn't say anything more.

The second unexpected event happened at the Big Bang Mountain ride. This time, Grandad let out a whopper of a fart that rattled the whole mountain and mining town, almost setting off a landslide! Everyone looked at Grandad,

"That wasn't me!" said Grandad.

"Yes, it was! I can't believe you'd lie!" said Alice.

"I think that fart at the Pirates of Atlantis was yours as well," said Grandma with a sly smile.

"That was you, Grandma!" said Alice, not quite believing how quickly Grandma was willing to shift the blame.

"You're a fart blamer!" said Grandad to Grandma.

"But you both farted! You're both as bad as each other!" said Alice, laughing.

That's when Mum and Dad came running up.

"We've just been on the Palace of Doom ride, and your Dad let off such a big fart they had to stop it and take everyone off!" said Mum, laughing.

"I didn't fart! It was you!" said Dad as Mum giggled.

"You're all as bad as each other! I can't believe it!" cried Alice.

"Now, Alice, we don't have much time left today. Is there anything else you'd like to see?" asked Grandad.

"The castle! I've not been to the castle yet. Please can we go there?" asked Alice.

"Yes, let's go, but I think that will be our last place to visit until next time," said Grandad.

And so, they all went to visit the Wonderland castle and had the most wonderful time.

Alice Appleby And The Kirkham Bum Blasters

11. THE SHORT FART HOME

The Applebys picked up their parachutes from the luggage storage, Grandad performed the final safety checks and, when the Applebys were ready, they each took a swig of the little glass vial containing Formula No. 2 Bum Blaster.

With a pop and a whoosh, they shot into the air, and it wasn't long before they were homeward bound. They flew back over Paris, past the Eiffel tower, and then along the River Seine, but not all was going as well as it seemed.

Over the English Channel, Grandma started to speed up.

"Come back, Grandma!" shouted Dad.

"I can't stop! I'm getting faster!" yelled Grandma as she let go of the rope and began to leave the rest of them behind.

"I hope she's not going supersonic!" said Dad as Grandma began to disappear in the distance.

"I don't think she's going that fast. I can still see her," said Mum.

"Maybe her bit of the formula had something extra in it," said Alice.

The Applebys watched on, helpless to do anything.

"At least she's heading in the right direction," said Dad as they crossed over the white cliffs of Dover and proceeded along the motorway.

Alice Appleby And The Kirkham Bum Blasters

"That's great! We can pick her up when we land!" said Dad as they approached the Appleby house.

"Time to deploy the parachutes!" said Grandad.

As they neared home, Mum yelled, "Look! I can see a parachute! Grandma's deployed in the next town across from us!"

One tug of the parachute cord and Alice, Mum, Dad, and Grandad all floated down to the back garden.

After packing up their parachutes, the Applebys made their way back to the house, but all was not well. Instead of the door being locked as they had left it, it was wide open, and what's worse, things had been taken from inside the Applebys house! Formula No. 3 Rocket Fuel was missing. So too, were the parachute presents for Uncle Paul and Auntie Lorri. What was even worse, Alice noticed The Kirkham Chili Super seeds were gone, along with her Notebook containing all the formulas from Auntie Kimberley!

"We've been broken into!" cried Dad, "And they've taken the Rocket Fuel!"

"Who would do such a thing?" said Grandad.

Lucky the Cat wandered into the kitchen with a Green Bowler hat in his mouth.

"Look! Lucky's brought us a clue!" said Grandad.

"I recognise that hat! It belongs to Gawk!" said Alice.

"Lady Blagdens manservant? Why would Gawk have been here?" said Grandad

"Maybe to deliver us another letter. I found this on the Kitchen table," said Mum, holding up a letter. The Applebys gathered around as Mum opened the letter and began to read.

> To whom it may concern,
> As explained in our letter earlier this year, you had a choice to either pay a fee for the continued use of the Blagden Estate land or, if you couldn't pay, we would take something away.
> You chose not to pay, so we took something away.
> Please don't come looking for it. It's ours now.
> Merry Christmas,
> The Blagden Estate

"The Blagdens have taken our Formula No. 3 rocket fuel!" said Mum.

"It's not *our* Formula No. 3. It's *NASA's* Formula," said Alice. But no one seemed to take note of what she said.

"They've taken Uncle Paul and Auntie Lorri' parachutes too" said Dad.

"They've taken my Super Seeds and my notebook!" said Alice.

"Oh, they aren't allowed to do that! It's stealing!" said Grandad.

"Let's go get them!" said Dad.

"What about Grandma? We can't leave her!" said Alice.

"I'll make sure Grandma gets home safely. You get Formula No. 3 back!" said Mum.

And with that, Alice, Dad, and Grandad set off for the Blagdens house on the hill.

12. MISSING FORMULA NO. 3

Grandad jumped into the car.

"Come on, both of you. We've got some villains to catch!"

Alice wasn't going to miss this for the world. She jumped into the back seat, while Dad got into the front passenger seat. They didn't have a chance to fasten their seatbelts before Grandad put the car in drive and sped along the road leading towards the Blagden's house on the hill.

"I can't believe they stole Bum Blaster No. 3! They've no right to just take what doesn't belong to them! They must have been watching us from up on the hill all this time," said Dad.

"Don't worry, we'll show them for stealing our Formula No. 3!" said Grandad.

"It's not *our* Formula No. 3. It's actually *NASA's* Formula No. 3," corrected Alice, but no one noticed.

The more worked up Grandad was getting, the faster they were going.

In no time at all, they found themselves by the Blagden's gate. Behind it, led a long driveway that snaked up the hill to the house Alice had seen through the telescope. Grandad stopped the car, and Dad jumped out to open the gate.

"It's no good, it's locked!" yelled Dad, rattling the gate.

Both Alice and Grandad got out of the car to take a closer look. While Dad and Grandad stood by the gate, Alice noticed a little nook in the hedgerow. She pushed on it gently, and it fell in, forming a gap.

"Look, there's a gap in the hedge! I think I can squeeze

through!" said Alice.

"Great work, Alice! See if you can get through!" said Dad. With one push, Alice fell through the gap and onto the snowy ground of the Blagden's property.

"I'm through! The gap's bigger than I thought!" said Alice.

"Okay, we're coming through," said Dad. First, Dad's head appeared through the gap, then came the rest of his body. Next, was Grandad's turn. His head, his shoulders, and then his belly came through the gap in the hedge.

"Right, let's go get them!" said Dad.

"Roger that," said Grandad. And with that, the Applebys started their march up the hill towards the Blagden's house. As they neared the house, the rear garden came into view. Lady Melantha Blagden stood in the middle on a wooden step with Gawk fussing around her. But wait, she had on a parachute! And so did Gawk! And Alices Packet of seeds and notebook were on a table right next to Formula No. 3!

"Those are Auntie Lorri's and Uncle Paul's parachutes!" said Alice.

That's when Gawk turned towards them.

"Hey, you! This is private property! Get off this land immediately or we shall call the police!" cried Gawk.

"You've stolen Formula No. 3! That's ours, and we're not leaving until you give it back!" said Dad.

"It's actually *NASA's* Formula No. 3," corrected Alice in a quiet voice.

"I've had enough of this! Give us our things back!" said Dad, marching towards Lady Blagden and Gawk.

Cool as a cucumber, Gawk produced a little, silver gun from his waistcoat pocket.

"Not so fast!" he said, pointing the gun at Dad.

Dad stopped dead in his tracks and put his hands up. Alice and Grandad raised their hands too.

That's when Lady Melantha turned to address them.

"I think you'll find we obtained the goods through the correct legal procedures. Your Formula No. 3 is now my Formula No. 3! Now, if you don't mind, I've some relatives in

Alice Appleby And The Kirkham Bum Blasters

Austria I plan to visit!"

"But that's not *our* Bum Blaster, that's *NASA's* No. 3 Rocket Fuel!" said Alice in a louder voice.

"Nonsense you little brat! I've seen first-hand what you have," snapped Lady Melantha.

"We've been watching you!" confirmed Gawk with a smirk, pointing at the telescope in the nearby house. Alice recognised the telescope. It was the same one she had seen from the Garden.

"Your Bum Blaster is a miracle, or should I say my Bum Blaster? When I grow those Kirkham chili seeds, everyone will want Bum Blaster! When people fly with Bum Blaster, it'll be cheaper and more convenient than using an airplane, and so much better for the environment! I'll be rich!"

"Rich!" echoed Gawk.

"Richer than you all, and I will buy the whole of England! I will be Queen, if that's what I wish, and bring you stupid, little simpletons under my rule, once and for all!" smiled Lady Melantha.

"Queen Melantha!" cried Gawk, looking up at her in awe.

"Let them have it," whispered Grandad to Alice and Dad.

"Are you sure? I don't fancy having Melantha as our Queen!" said Dad.

"I'm sure. Somehow, I don't think she will ever be our Queen. Also, if it is NASA's Rocket Bum Blaster, it would be best if we weren't around when they drink the formula and turn into human rockets! Now, if we could just sneak off and leave them ..." whispered Grandad, but he was interrupted before he could finish.

"What are you whispering?" snapped Gawk, collecting himself and pointing the gun at them with a look of suspicion.

"Oh, we were just saying, Your Majesty, that If you think it's your Bum Blaster, you might as well have it and use it as you wish," said Dad.

Lady Blagden smiled victoriously. "Quite right! I knew you'd come to your senses. There's no denying that when you simpletons knew I was going to be your ruler, you wouldn't question me further. You couldn't! Now, come on Gawk. Let's get our royal bums moving!"

"Yes, Your Majesty! Coming, Your Majesty!" crowed Gawk. He strapped on his parachute, and he and the Lady each took a big swig of Formula No. 3.

"To Austria!" cried the Lady triumphantly.

"Quick, let's get out of here!" said Grandad, and with that, the Applebys took off down the hill.

Alice could swear she heard numbers being counted down from somewhere.

"5 … 4 … 3 … 2 … 1… "

As Alice, Grandad, and Dad reached the gate at the bottom of the hill, two gigantic rocket booms rang out one after the other! Although they were a little distance away, Alice could clearly see everything happening at the top of the hill.

BRRRROOMMMM!!

"WAH, WAH, WAH!" yelled Lady Melantha flapping her arms frantically, and in a flash, she shot one thousand feet high into the air, flames leaping from her backside!

Gawk wasn't far behind; this time, his arms were flapping like a sped-up duck. He too, had flames shooting out of his bottom!

BRRRROOMMMM!!

The smoke that emanated out from their bottoms left tremendous, black, billowing clouds that covered the entire Blagden house!

"Do you think they'll make it to Austria?" asked Alice innocently.

"Austria? They're going so fast, they're more likely to land in Australia!" said Dad.

"Australia? Judging by their trajectory, it's more likely to be an Asteroid!" said Grandad looking up.

The Applebys followed the black vapor trails, watching Lady Melantha and Gawk getting smaller and smaller in the sky until they were little more than tiny, black dots in the distance.

"Come on, my neck's beginning to hurt," said Grandad.

"Hold on! I need to get my notebook and the Kirkham Bum Blaster seeds they took!" said Alice. Before Dad or Grandad could stop her, Alice ran back up the hill, through the smoke, and to the table. There she found her notebook and the little packet of seeds she had made. Then she came running back down the hill to Grandad and Dad.

Then they all squeezed back through the hole in the Blagdens hedge and went home.

13. MOONLINGS

The stars twinkled and winkled against the fabric of night. With not a cloud in the sky, the moon shone clear and bright.

It was another hunter's moon, and Lucky the Cat could not be called in. The cold had a way of pulling you back indoors to the warmth, yet two of the Applebys had ventured out into the night.

"Can you see it?" asked Grandad, looking up to the sky.

"Almost. It's moving fast again," said Alice, peering through the eyepiece of the telescope. Her little, cold hands turned the adjustment wheels, searching for focus. With a final twist, the view through the telescope sharpened, and for a while, she gazed.

"Well, do you see the craters?" asked Grandad.

"Yes, I do, but there's something different," said Alice.

"Different? How so?" asked Grandad.

"You know how you said the moon is made of cheese and, instead of colour, has only light and dark?"

"Yes, Alice, I do," said Grandad with a chuckle.

"Well, there's something I think you should see."

Grandad stopped smiling and took over for Alice, peering through the telescope. There, on the moon, were what looked like two tiny, little people in the middle of a newly-formed crater. One wore a maroon dress, and the other, a smaller person, was dressed in green. The tiny people had an uncanny resemblance to Lady Melantha Blagden and Gawk.

Alice Appleby And The Kirkham Bum Blasters

Grandad and Alice looked at one another, their mouths open in disbelief.

"It can't be!" said Grandad.

"It is!" said Alice. "Kirkham's Bum Blasters No. 3 sent them both to the moon!"

Grandad peered back through the telescope for a second look, and then he turned to Alice. "It is them," he said, looking a little confused, as if not sure what to do.

"At least the man on the moon won't be lonely anymore," said Alice with a smile.

"No, I suppose not!" said Grandad, with a chuckle.

They both grinned, then giggled, then laughed until tears began to roll down their cheeks!

Alice pulled the telescope close to take another look, but the moon had already moved on. Before she could refocus the telescope, Mum called from the kitchen. "Alice, Grandad, your hot chocolate is ready. Come in before you catch your death of cold!"

Reluctantly, they went inside and sat by the fire, sipping their hot chocolate and sharing the occasional grin.

"What are you smiling about?" asked Grandma suspiciously, looking at the two of them.

"Oh, just a little something we saw far away on the moon," said Grandad with a smirk.

Alice almost burst out laughing. Neither Grandad nor Alice told another soul about the two little people they saw on the moon that night. It was their secret, and besides, even if they told anyone, who would believe them?

After the hot chocolate was finished and the fire began to dim, Alice went to bed, tucked herself up in the big duvet, and had the best night's sleep ever.

The   End.

Thank you for buying this book!

I hope you enjoyed meeting Alice and the rest of the Applebys? Did you know Leaving a reader review is super important to an Author like me? It also helps other kids like you discover great books to read too!

So if you liked this story, please consider:

1. Telling your Friends
2. Leave a review on Amazon or Good Reads
3. Telling me, I'd love to hear from you!

www.facebook.com/nbfletcherauthor

www.instagram.com/nbfletcherauthor

www.nbfletcher.com

Alice Appleby And The Kirkham Bum Blasters

Printed in Great Britain
by Amazon

8055614d-59b9-47b6-a958-fafe7f0af1c0R01